T0149063

THE PHILOSOPHY OF
CHEESE

THE PHILOSOPHY OF
CHEESE

PATRICK McGUIGAN

First published 2020 by
The British Library
96 Euston Road
London NW1 2DB

Text copyright © Patrick McGuigan 2020
Illustrations copyright © British Library Board 2020
and other named copyright holders

ISBN 978 0 7123 5377 9
eISBN 978 0 7123 6722 6
Cataloguing in Publication Data
A catalogue record for this book is available
from the British Library

Designed and typeset by Sandra Friesen
Printed and bound in the Czech Republic by Finidr

CONTENTS

INTRODUCTION

Every time I see a well-stocked cheese counter I still marvel that everything in there is made, more or less, with one main ingredient. From vast, grainy drums of Parmesan and gooey rounds of Brie to craggy blues and sticky, orange cheeses that smell foul but taste glorious, they all started life as milk. That there are literally thousands of different cheeses made around the world in a kaleidoscope of shapes, sizes, colours, textures and flavours is testament to the ingenuity and imagination of people, who keep coming up with new ways of turning milk into things that taste delicious. It's been going on for the best part of 8,000 years and we still haven't run out of new ideas, which is frankly mind-boggling.

Food has always been a way to understand the world, but this is especially true of cheese, which has played such a central role in diets over such a long period that it can be used like a window through which to view history, geography and culture. There's a great quote from the estimable cheese writer Patrick Rance about this: 'A slice of good

CHEESE—1 Gorgonzola. 2 Double Gloucester. 3 Koboko. 4 Parmesan. 5 Dutch. 6 Roquefort. 7 Schabzieger. 8 Dunragit. 9 York Cream. 10 Port du Salut. 11 Cheddar. 12 Pommel. 13 Camembert. 14 Mainzer 15 Cheshire. 16 Stilton. 17 Cream Bondon. 18 Gruyere. 19 Wiltshire Loaf. 20 Cheddar Loaf.

cheese is never just a thing to eat,' he wrote in *The French Cheese Book*, published in 1989.[1] 'It is usually also a slice of local history: agricultural, political, or ecclesiastical.' He could have added that cheese can also be a wedge of social, economic, military or intellectual history with a good smattering of art, literature, science and myth thrown in for good measure. Trying to cram all of that into a slim volume would have been a futile task, but by telling the stories of some of the most famous cheeses of the Western world, and how they came about and evolved over time, we can open a window onto some of these slices of human life down the centuries with a few rollicking good stories along the way.

The decision to focus mainly on cheese in the West was not taken lightly. From paneer in India to queso blanco in Mexico, there are plenty of fascinating cheese tales to be found outside Europe and the US, but they often have their origins in Europe or are not as central to their respective food cultures as in the West. The cheeses chosen for this book all have something to say about particular places and periods of history, as well as demonstrating how cheese-making has evolved and adapted to fit the times, from the very first curd to industrial block Cheddar. Think of it as an epic cheeseboard through time and space.

You could also quite easily buy the cheeses featured in the book and build your own real cheeseboard to nibble as you read. The philosophy of cheese is all well and good, but eating it is better (see pages 89–94).

HOW CHEESE IS MADE

Before we plunge into thousands of years of cheese adventures, it's probably worth laying out the fundamentals of how cheese is made. In some ways, it's an incredibly simple foodstuff. In other ways, it's endlessly complex and hard to get your head around.

The first thing to understand is that cheese is a fermented food. Like brewers use yeast to make beer, cheesemakers rely on bacteria to turn milk into cheese. Add the right ones to milk (or let them grow naturally) and these micro-organisms feed on the milk sugars (lactose) and create lactic acid. Raising the acidity helps preservation because it creates an environment that makes it harder for harmful bacteria to grow, but it also plays a part in the transformation of milk from a liquid to a wobbly blancmange-like curd. An enzyme found in the stomachs of goat kids, lambs and calves called chymosin, but better known as rennet, which curdles milk, is also usually added to speed up this process and create a firmer curd, but not always. The other essential element of cheese is salt, which inhibits the lactic acid bacteria once they've done their job, helps with preservation and adds flavour.

These are the basic ingredients of almost all cheeses, but there are plenty of other steps you can take in the dairy and maturing room to end up with very different outcomes.

You can play around with acidity and salt levels to achieve different textures and flavours. The technique of cutting the curd allows water trapped in the delicate structure to be released in the form of whey. The more you cut, the drier your curd, and the firmer your final cheese. You can also 'scald' the cut curd in hot whey and pile it up after the whey has drained (known as cheddaring) to further reduce moisture content. Pressing the curd in moulds is another technique to squeeze out whey and create a harder cheese that can be aged for longer, such as Cheddar or Gruyère. You can even pull and stretch curd in hot water to create an elastic cheese like Mozzarella.

Then there's stuff you can do as a cheese matures, such as encouraging particular bacteria, moulds and yeasts to grow on the rind or within the cheese itself, or ageing it for a long time, all of which will have an impact on appearance, flavour and texture. And finally, let's not forget the milk itself. As you might expect, depending on whether you use the milk of goats, sheep, cows, buffaloes, yaks, reindeer, horses, camels or even donkeys, you will end up with a very different cheese. The actual breed of the animal has an impact too, while milk also changes throughout the season, influenced by factors such as the weather, the animal's lactation cycle and even what time of the day it is milked. Likewise, diet plays an important role in milk composition. A cow grazing Alpine summer pastures in Switzerland, filled with wild grasses, herbs and flowers, will produce very different milk for cheesemaking to one that has been fed on turnips and silage in a winter shed in Scotland.

I sometimes feel a bit sorry for cheesemakers, who have to work with an ingredient that changes from one day to the next and often misbehaves, but it's also what makes cheese such a fascinating and endlessly varied food. Through skill, patience and hard work cheesemakers have learned over thousands of years to take an unruly natural product and transform it into something else completely.

CURD

We don't know precisely when and where the first person decided to see what the lumpy bits in curdled milk tasted like, but it was probably around 8,000 years ago in the Middle East. It must have been a surprisingly pleasant discovery. Leave milk for long enough in the right conditions and it spontaneously starts to sour and thicken into yoghurt, as natural bacteria convert the milk sugars into lactic acid and cause the milk to curdle. Tasting its refreshing tang and comforting milky flavours for the first time would have been a mini-revelation – one that might have prompted our brave Neolithic taster to go back for a second try and perhaps even offer some to whomever happened to be nearby. It wouldn't have taken much for them to experiment by draining off some of the liquid whey and adding a sprinkle of salt to leave a basic soft curd. And so the world's first ever cheese was born.

Remarkably, cheese is still made in a similar way today. Labneh, which is produced by straining yoghurt through cloth until you are left with a creamy cheese, is still a staple of Middle Eastern cuisine, often drizzled with olive oil and scattered with herbs, or dried to make hard balls of yoghurt cheese called jameed. In the warm climate of the Middle East it wouldn't have taken long for milk to naturally sour and curdle, but the process could have been aided by using rennet. Nobody knows for certain when the curdling powers of rennet were first discovered, but one theory is that Neolithic people would have spotted solidified milk in the stomachs of slaughtered kids and lambs, and started to experiment. Another is that they tried to store milk in dried animal stomachs and found that the enzyme naturally present in the improvised pouches transformed the liquid milk into curd. What is more certain is that this happened in an area called the Fertile Crescent, which stretched in a crescent shape from the Nile Valley up through Syria to southern Turkey and then down through what is now Iraq and parts of Iran.

The area, which is also known as the Cradle of Civilisation, underwent a significant change in climatic conditions around 9500 BCE, resulting in warmer temperatures and more stable seasons, allowing inhabitants to abandon their previous nomadic hunter-gatherer ways in favour of permanent settlements where they could cultivate crops. This was the start of the Neolithic revolution, and it wasn't long before these first farms attracted naturally curious wild goats and sheep. The first evidence of people domesticating these animals comes from around 8500 BCE in the foothills of the Taurus Mountains of southern Turkey and the Zagros Mountains of western Iran.[2] It was only a matter of time before these early farmers started messing around with their milk. Sure enough, dairy residues have been found on pottery sherds in the Fertile Crescent dating back to the seventh millennium BCE,[3] while the first definitive evidence of cheesemaking came in the form of pieces of pottery with small holes, dating from 7,500 years ago.

Initially, archaeologists were puzzled as to what these strange bits of perforated clay pots, found at various Neolithic sites, might have been used for. Some thought they were possibly for straining honey or some kind of fire brazier. But one young American archaeologist, Peter Bogucki, was convinced they had been used as a sieve or strainer for draining whey from cheese, after spotting a similar-looking nineteenth-century cheese mould at a friend's house.[4] This was back in the 1980s, but the only problem was that there was no way of proving his theory.

Nearly 30 years later, biochemistry finally caught up with Bogucki's hypothesis, with new testing techniques developed by the University of Bristol able to extract and analyse residues trapped within pottery sherds found at a site in Poland, dating back to 5500 BCE. These showed that the residues were dairy fats – a 'smoking gun' that confirmed the funny pots with holes were indeed cheese strainers used for separating whey from curd.[5] Incidentally, scientists at

the University of York have had great fun making Neolithic cheese strainers from clay to see if they actually work in practice – and sure enough they have been able to make fresh curd that wouldn't look out of place on the menu in a restaurant in Istanbul or Baghdad, or even London or New York, today.[6]

Happy days for our Neolithic cheesemakers, but beyond just tasting nice and kick-starting thousands of years of dairy history, these first cheeses were also important in terms of human survival and evolution by allowing prehistoric people to preserve milk for longer and make it more transportable. Cheese also made milk easier to digest, which gave them an evolutionary advantage. Babies and infants are able to digest lactose – the sugar in milk – thanks to the production of an enzyme called lactase, but genetic research has shown that early Stone Age people stopped producing lactase after infancy, which meant that all adults

during this period were lactose intolerant. Drinking fresh, liquid milk would have given people terrible stomach aches, wind and worse. However, milk turns sour and starts to curdle because natural bacteria metabolise the lactose. Strain off the whey to make cheese and you have a dairy product that is much lower in lactose, and therefore much easier to stomach. This remains true today – cheese contains zero or vanishingly small amounts of lactose, which is good news for lactose-intolerant cheese lovers.[7]

In fact, most people in the West can happily drink milk now because centuries of dairy consumption has led to a genetic mutation which means they continue to produce lactase into adulthood (known as lactase persistence). On the other hand, populations of countries without strong dairy traditions, including large swathes of East and South East Asia, and sub-Saharan Africa, continue to be lactose intolerant.

A word of warning about the theory that lactose intolerance in Neolithic people was an important driver in the invention of cheese: scientists are starting to revise this idea, partly because there is growing evidence that people who are lactose intolerant can actually drink milk quite happily without feeling ill. Dairy science is invariably complicated. It may be that Stone Age people were able to drink milk and therefore developed cheese as a way of preserving it for longer (and because it tasted good). What is true is that cheese was a new, highly nutritious foodstuff for Neolithic people that would have helped them survive and thrive. As the population in the Fertile Crescent grew, people began to move further afield, slowly migrating into Asia, North Africa and Europe, taking their cheesemaking know-how with them, and developing it further along the way.

Dairy farming had reached Spain by 5400 BCE and Britain by 4000 BCE, while there is evidence of cheese-making in Egypt in 3000 BCE, India in 1500 BCE and Mongolia in 1300 BCE.[8] In Mesopotamia (Southern Iraq) the Sumerian civilisation, which dates back to 4000 BCE, had descriptions for at least 20 distinct cheeses, including white cheese, fresh cheese, rich cheese and sharp cheese.[9]

In one of the myths of the Sumerian goddess Inanna, a clever shepherd wins her hand in marriage with the gifts of cheese, butter and yoghurt. Daily offerings of ewes' milk cheeses and butter were made at temples in the Sumerian city-state of Uruk in tribute to Inanna, spawning large farming and dairy production operations. The number of daily cheese offerings at the temples grew to such an extent that the priests had to come up with a new accounting system to keep track of them. Symbols were scratched into wet clay as cheeses and other offerings were delivered to the temples in what was an early forerunner of cuneiform, one of the first sytems of writing.[10]

From that first experimental cheese somewhere in the Fertile Crescent to helping to establish the first script, cheese had come a long way. But the story was only just beginning.

FETA

Digging up ancient pottery cheese strainers is one thing. Finding actual cheese that is more than 3,000 years old in an Egyptian tomb is quite another. That's what happened in 2014 during an excavation of a tomb in Saqqara, Egypt, that belonged to Ptahmes, mayor of the ancient city of Memphis and a high-ranking official under successive pharaohs. In one of the tomb's chambers archaeologists found a collection of broken jars, one of which contained an unknown white substance covered by a cloth. Intrigued, scientists analysed the matter and found it was a 3,200-year-old cheese, which might have been left as a snack for the afterlife. Any thoughts of actually trying the ancient dairy product, which was made from a mix of sheep's, goat's and cow's milk, were quickly dismissed when they detected it also contained bacteria that could cause brucellosis – an infectious disease that can lead to fever, diarrhoea, an enlarged spleen and death.[11]

Beyond being a good story, which made headlines around the world, the fact that the Saqqara cheese contained cow's milk and was preserved in ceramic jars shows how farming and cheese techniques were evolving. As cheese became ingrained in people's lives during the Bronze Age from 3300 to 1200 BCE, and the subsequent Iron Age, which lasted to around 500 BCE, new tools and production methods began to surface. Ricotta-style cheeses were developed by heating milk in special ceramic milk boilers, while the use of rennet to make firmer curd that could be pressed and aged for longer became widespread.

We know for sure that rennet was being used in the second millennium BCE. Records from the Hittite civilisation, which grew up in what is now Turkey, include direct references to rennet and 'aged soldier cheeses',[12] while bronze cheese graters have been discovered in Italy and Crete dating back to 1100 BCE, which could only have been used with hard cheeses, set with rennet. There's even a reference to cheese graters in the *Iliad*, which was written around 800 BCE. Nestor is revived after a hard day at the siege of Troy with a glass of wine infused with honey into which hard goat's cheese is grated and sprinkled with barley meal. As cocktail recipes go, it's not going to rival the Manhattan anytime soon, but it does show how cheese was viewed as a healthy, nutritious food.

New storage methods were also developed, such as packing cheese into ceramic pots so it would keep better (as demonstrated by the Egyptian tomb cheese) and could be traded and even shipped. Pot cheeses are still found in

Iran and Turkey today, where salted curd is packed into a ceramic amphora called a *kupa* (Iran) or *carra* (Turkey) and the top sealed with vine leaves or cloth, before being buried upside down at depths of up to six feet for up to six months.

Whey would have naturally leaked from cheeses left in pots, mixing with the added salt to create brine, which would have helped keep the cheeses even longer. It's thought that Bronze Age cheesemakers then started to make their own brine as a preservative in which to submerge their cheese. Pickled cheeses like this are still made in Eastern Europe, the Balkans, the Middle East and North

Africa, but the most famous of all is Feta from Greece, which is made from ewe's and goat's milk and is aged in brine for up to a year.

A cheese that many believe is a forerunner of Feta is described in great detail in Homer's *Odyssey*, written around the same period as the *Iliad*. Odysseus and his crew land on an island (possibly modern-day Sicily or the Greek island of Chios), where they discover the cave of Polyphemus, the giant Cyclops.

'We soon reached his cave, but he was out shepherding, so we went inside and took stock of all that we could see. His cheese-racks were loaded with cheeses, and he had more lambs and kids than his pens could hold. They were kept in separate flocks; first there were the hoggets, then the oldest of the younger lambs and lastly the very young ones all kept apart from one another; as for his dairy, all the vessels, bowls, and milk pails into which he milked, were swimming with whey.'[13]

There's also a useful description of how the one-eyed cheesemaker goes about his craft, when he returns, watched by the hidden sailors, who are trapped in the cave after the giant seals up the entrance with a huge stone behind him.

'When he had so done he sat down and milked his ewes and goats, all in due course, and then let each of them have her own young. He curdled half the milk and set it aside in wicker strainers, but the other half he poured into bowls that he might drink it for his supper.'

After munching a few of Odysseus's crew, the story doesn't end well for the poor giant – Odysseus thrusts a stake into his eye and escapes clinging to the underside of a sheep – but it does provide useful clues to how cheese was made nearly 3,000 years ago. Polyphemus uses some kind of rennet to curdle his milk quickly – possibly fig sap or animal rennet – and the curd is drained and possibly pressed in wicker baskets, before being set on racks to dry. This may have been to make a hard aged cheese, but the fact that the Cyclops carefully keeps his whey suggests he may have used it to make a brine for a Feta-style cheese.

Known as *τυρί* in ancient Greece, which simply translates as 'cheese', then *prosphatos* in the Middle Ages, Feta got its current name in the seventeenth century after the word for 'slice'. While most Feta is now brined in beechwood barrels or metal tanks, it was common for the cheese to be stored and transported in ceramic pots well into the last century.

Feta is still a staple in Greece today (the EU's Protected Food Names scheme lays down in law that it can't be made anywhere else), made with sheep's and up to 30 per cent goat's milk, much of it on a large scale for supermarket shelves. It tends to be aged in brine for just a few months and is mild, salty and crumbly. But Feta that has spent six to 12 months maturing in brine-filled beechwood barrels has a much tangier, complex flavour, taking in fruity, herbaceous and even animal notes. Ask a Greek how to eat it, and they'll invariably recommend it served with watermelon and mint.

That cheese appears in the *Iliad* and the *Odyssey*, and a growing number of varieties were being made and traded in the Bronze and Iron Ages, shows just how central it had become to people's lives. But cheese was much more than an everyday snack. As we saw with the Sumerians, who gave it as a temple offering, cheese was an important part of rituals and ceremonies during this period. The Spartan poet Alcman, who lived around 700 BCE, sang of how 'a great cheese, whole and unbroken and shining white' would be made with 'the milk of a lioness' as part of torch-lit festivals to honour the gods.[14] Around the same period, Spartan youths would have to 'steal' cheese from the Temple of Artemis Orthia, the goddess of fertility and childbirth, while also trying to avoid being whipped by guards as part of a coming-of-age ritual that sounds like an early version of *The Hunger Games* with cheese.[15]

Over in Neolithic England, cheese was considered to be such a special food by the builders of Stonehenge that it played an important part in huge religious feasts, according to researchers at the UCL Institute of Archaeology. They analysed 4,500-year-old pot fragments from the Durrington Walls settlement, where the constructors of Stonehenge are thought to have lived, and found that the vessels were likely to have been used to store curds and whey or cottage cheese. The pots were kept in special ceremonial buildings, while other foods were found all over, suggesting that cheese had a rarefied status, perhaps as a marker of social status or as a symbol of purity and ritual significance.[16]

Even more remarkable, during excavations of Xiaohe Cemetery in Xinjiang, Western China, immaculately preserved mummies, entombed around 3,500 years ago, were found with little nuggets of cheese carefully placed around their necks and chests – the oldest intact cheese ever found. One of the mummies, nicknamed the Beauty of Xiaohe because of her high cheekbones, flaxen hair and beautiful eyelashes, also had a fertility symbol in the shape of a wooden phallus on her chest, indicating that cheese was perhaps somehow connected to the idea of rebirth and renewal.[17]

Whatever the reason, it's clear that cheese held a special place in early civilisations. A position that would only strengthen with the rise of the Romans.

PECORINO

As the Egyptian and Greek civilisations waned, the Roman Republic rose, and with it came a wealth of written material detailing how cheese was made and its importance in Roman life. From the fifth century BCE onwards, the Roman Republic and later Empire expanded at a rapid rate, first taking control of the Italian peninsula, before colonising much of the rest of Europe in a series of bloody wars and conquests. As Rome's wealth and power grew, so did demand for food, leading to the creation of large farming estates, known as *latifundia*, producing grain, olive oil and wine. Sheep were also raised for wool and meat, and were prized for their rich milk, which was turned into hard, aged cheeses that would have looked and tasted a lot like the Pecorino cheeses made in Italy today ('Pecorino' derives from the Italian word for sheep: *pecora*).

Much of our knowledge of Roman cheeses comes from agricultural writers, such as Cato and Varro, whose work is a treasure trove of clues and insights into how cheese was made more than 2,000 years ago. One of the most

detailed accounts of cheesemaking can be found in a farming manual called *De Re Rustica* (On Agriculture), written around 60 CE by Lucius Junius Moderatus Columella, a Spaniard who served in the Roman army, before running several farms in Italy. He recommends 'rich and thick' milk for longer-aged cheeses, set with lamb's or kid's rennet, although he does detail other plant-based alternatives, including fig sap and the seeds of a thistle called safflower, plus the flowers of wild thistles. The stamen of a thistle called cardoon is still used by some cheesemakers today to set milk, especially in Spain and Portugal in soft, pungent 'torta' cheeses.

Columella also records how cheesemakers used weights to press the cheeses into moulds or wicker baskets to help squeeze out whey, before being salted. The cheese was then aged by being 'closely packed on several shelves in an enclosed place which is not exposed to the winds'. This sounds remarkably like a maturing room to me, and the process is very similar to how Pecorino is still made today in Italy, where there are numerous regional versions of the cheese, many of which are protected under the same laws that cover Feta.

It's probably worth quickly explaining the Protected Food Names scheme in a bit more detail, which covers

many of Europe's best-known cheeses. Launched by the
EU in 1992, it grew from the appellation system for wine
and lays down in law where and how traditional foods can
be made, with qualifying products covered by a Protected
Designation of Origin (PDO) or the less strict Protected
Geographical Indication (PGI). It means that PDO-
protected Pecorino Sardo, for example, can only be made
in Sardinia with sheep's milk, although it's worth noting
the laws are not recognised by all countries outside the
EU, which has led to some bitter trade disputes with the
US. Romano, Toscano, Sardo and Siciliano are the best
known of Italy's eight PDO Pecorinos, which can only

be made in their respective areas with specifications on everything from what the animal eats to the size and age of the cheese. Each has its own characteristics, but mature Pecorino cheeses tend to be hard, grainy, salty and piquant, often with a savoury, sheepy flavour. They're great with a drizzle of honey.

Other types of Roman cheese were referenced in Columella's writing, including fresh cheese 'to be eaten within a few days', which was flavoured with pine nuts or thyme, and hard, brined cheese that was smoked with applewood. Today we would call these 'flavour-added' cheeses – a category that has seen its reputation tarnished in modern times (in the UK at least) by the creation of abominations such as Thai Curry Cheddar and Eggnog-flavoured Wensleydale. Fresh sheep's cheese with crushed pine nuts, on the other hand, sounds quite nice.

Another intriguing product, described in *De Re Rustica*, was 'hand pressed cheese', which involved breaking up the curd and submerging it in hot water before shaping it by hand or pressing it into wooden box moulds. This sounds suspiciously similar to how Mozzarella is made. There's also a strange section on how to cure an ox with stomach troubles that involves cheese. The first advice is to show the poorly animal a duck – a sight that will result in it being 'quickly delivered from its torment' – but if that doesn't work, feeding the beast a concoction of pounded-up pine cones, acorns, 'rough wine' and 'very old cheese' should do the trick.

Politician and landowner Marcus Porcius Cato, who preceded Columella by a few hundred years, was also interested in cheese recipes, although not for oxen. In his farming handbook *De Agricultura* (On Farming), he included details of an epic Roman cheesecake called 'placenta', which contained 6.4 kg (14 lbs) of soft sheep's milk cheese and 2 kg (4½ lbs) of honey, which were layered in a vast pastry case measuring one foot by two feet. This was baked in a clay dish with a lid, buried in hot coals, before the pastry was served hot with even more honey to create what he modestly describes as 'a half-modius cake'. Other recipes from the book included fried cheese fritters called 'globi', covered in honey and poppy seeds – a kind of sweet cheese doughnut – plus a cheese loaf called 'libum', often given as an offering to the gods.

First-century general and historian Pliny the Elder listed the 'most esteemed' cheeses of Rome, in his 37-book tome *Natural History*, referencing a 'fresh tasting' cheese from parts of Nemausus (Nîmes) in Gaul – a region that is best known today for Roquefort – and a cheese with a 'saltish flavour' from Bithynia (a Roman province that corresponds to northern Turkey), which was considered 'first in quality' of all overseas cheeses. This could perhaps be a Feta-style brined cheese.

Another intriguing cheese mentioned by Pliny was Luna, which came from the frontiers of Etruria in central Italy and Liguria in the northwest. These cheeses were 'remarkable for their vast size, a single cheese weighing as much as a thousand pounds'. The poet Martial also marvelled at the huge size of Luna, which was stamped with a moon impression and would 'afford your slaves a thousand lunches'. These are surely exaggerations – a half-tonne cheese was not exactly practical before the invention of forklift trucks – but it's clear that Luna was an unusually large specimen. By their nature, really big cheeses require low moisture content so they can be aged for a long time without rotting at their cores. To make the mighty mountain cheeses of today, such as Emmental, which can weigh up to 100 kg (220 lbs), and Bergkäse, which is made in 60 kg (132 lb) wheels, cheesemakers use different techniques to reduce moisture, such as cutting the curd into tiny pieces, scalding (cooking) them at very high temperatures and then pressing them hard to squeeze out whey.

There's no record of how Luna was made, but cheese writer Paul Kindstedt argues that its shear size suggests there's a chance that some or all of these techniques were being used.[18] This would mean that as well as perfecting Pecorino, developing flavoured cheeses and inventing cheese doughnuts, the Romans may also have made the first 'cooked', hard-pressed cheeses, which were early forerunners of Gruyère, Comté and Parmesan. It turns out the Romans did quite a lot for us when it comes to cheese.

MUNSTER

VISIT THE foothills of the Vosges mountains in Alsace-Lorraine at the end of May, and the air will be filled with the clank of cow bells and the buzz of excited cheesemakers. It's at this time that the region's dairy farmers, known as *marcaires* (milkers), lead their speckled black and white Vosgienne cows up into high mountain pastures (the *chaumes*) for the summer. Here the animals graze on stubble fields and produce particularly delicious milk that is perfect for cheesemaking.

Historically the marcaires would stay with their animals throughout the summer, making a cheese called Munster with the sweet milk in stone chalets, only returning in the autumn, in a tradition known as transhumance – a way of farming that is at the heart of many mountain cheeses, from Emmental and Fontina to Beaufort and Ossau-Iraty. Times have changed, and fewer cheesemakers now live in the mountains during the summer, but the ascent (and descent) is still a big deal in this part of northeastern France. The hardy cows are garlanded in flowers, and the marcaires dress up in traditional clothes (a leather cap is essential) as part of festivals celebrating their passage up and down the mountains.

The reason for all the fuss is that Munster is one of the oldest, most famous and smelliest cheeses on the planet. A soft frisbee-shaped cheese, it has a sticky orange rind so pungent that it's hard not to think of sweaty socks when you catch a whiff. But if you're brave enough to take a bite, the eating experience is very different. The soft, buttery paste balances out the rind so that it's pleasantly rich, spicy and meaty. It's a great example of what is known as a washed-rind cheese. The rind is smeared with brine in the maturing room to encourage particularly smelly bacteria, yeasts and moulds to grow, which give the exterior an orangey-red hue and the cheese its pronounced flavour. It's a technique that was mastered by monks in medieval abbeys across Europe, including in the Vosges mountains, where a monastery called Saint-Gregoire was first built in the seventh century and later became known as Munster after an early word for 'monastery'.[19]

We left our story with the Romans in the previous chapter, but even the best Pecorino and Luna cheeses weren't enough to save the empire from collapse. By 476 CE the Western Roman Empire had fallen at the hands of the German 'barbarians', signalling the beginning of the Middle Ages. Much of Europe was carved up into a patchwork of different kingdoms, with the Germanic

MARCAIRES DE LA MONTAGNE.

invaders expanding Roman villas and estates into manors, comprising the lord's own personal farm (the demesne), plus separate peasant smallholdings and villages, which would of course pay for the privilege of living on the manor.

Between the fifth and seventh centuries, Christianity became the guiding religion across Gaul and Britain as the Franks and the Anglo-Saxons slowly gave up their pagan ways. This was important for cheese because Germanic lords with land to spare were enthusiastic supporters in the creation of monasteries, which became centres of cheesemaking knowledge and innovation.

The German aristocrat Boniface, the Duke of Alsace, helped a group of Irish monks, who followed the teachings of St Columbanus, to set up Munster Abbey in 660 CE.

This initial strain of Irish monasticism was eventually surpassed and subsumed by a different order, which followed the teachings of St Benedict. An obscure Italian abbott who lived from 480–543 CE, St Benedict preached that work was an important part of spiritual life, with monks expected to 'live by the labour of their hands', and idleness decreed 'the enemy of the soul'.[20]

Hundreds of Benedictine monasteries were set up across Europe in the seventh and eighth centuries, with another wave of Cistercian monasteries from the twelfth century. Boom time for monasteries also meant boom time for cheese, with monks and lay brothers living by the labour of their hands by cultivating land and making their own food and drink, including cheese, beer and wine. Monastery lands were also rented to local dairy farmers, who would pay part of their rent in milk or in cheeses they had made themselves. This was the case at Munster Abbey, where the monks let out pastures in the Vosges mountains to the marcaires, who would supply the monastery with milk and cheese in return, but also make cheese for themselves on both the Alsace and Lorraine sides of the mountains. These high-altitude cheesemakers, working at 900–1400 m (2,950–4,600 ft) above sea level, had to carve out the pastures themselves by clearing mountain valleys of trees and bushes to create meadows and fields that could be harvested for hay and used for grazing their animals. To think that cows are still being taken up to these very same pastures, hewn from the landscape more than 1,000 years ago and tended ever since, is quite remarkable.[21]

Many of the most famous cheeses in the world have their roots in monasteries, including Époisses de Bourgogne, Maroilles and Pont-l'Évêque, which like Munster are washed-rind cheeses with similar funky orange exteriors. It's no coincidence that these soft cheeses all come from northern France, where the cool climate and damp stone cellars of monasteries would have combined to create an environment that naturally encouraged the pungent bacteria (called *Brevibacterium linens*) to grow on the rinds. Incidentally, the same bacteria grow on human skin and particularly like the warm, damp space between your toes. It's no coincidence that washed-rind cheeses sometimes have a distinct aroma of sweaty socks, and why, in turn, some feet smell cheesy.

It wouldn't have taken much for our cheesemaking monks and farmers to learn that by wiping the cheeses with brine, or brine mixed with a dash of alcohol, it would help the process along, and make them even more full-flavoured. Époisses is washed in a solution containing Marc de Bourgogne – a brandy distilled from Burgundy wine grape pomace – creating a wonderful terracotta-coloured, wrinkly rind that is almost psychedelic in the intensity of its smell. Legend has it that it was used in trials of ordeal in the Middle Ages. If the accused choked on the powerful cheese it was a sure sign of guilt.

The influence of stinky cheeses invented by men of the cloth in the Middle Ages can still be felt today with numerous modern washed-rind cheeses. The Wallace and Gromit favourite, Stinking Bishop, has been made in Gloucestershire since 1994 and is washed with brine and perry (the cheese is named after the pear variety that is used to make the pear cider). Cheesemaker Charles Martell was inspired to make the cheese after learning that his land was once farmed by Cistercian monks. Going full circle from the Irish monks who first set up Munster Abbey, Ireland is also a hotbed of washed-rind cheesemaking today. Its damp, briny climate provides the perfect environment for maturing pungent cheeses, such as Milleens, Gubbeen and Durrus.

Back in Munster, the famous abbey has long since stopped producing cheese. Damaged by fire and war over the centuries, it was closed in 1791 and only ruins now remain, some of which have been turned into a snack bar with natty pink chairs among the vestiges of the once great order. Thankfully, Munster cheese is on the menu.

The monks' cheesemaking know-how lives on, however, with around sixty producers still making the region's most famous cheese, many of them small-scale, farmhouse (*fermier*) producers. Some of these mountain farms have been turned into hotels and inns, where hikers can stay and enjoy a 'marcaire meal' of Munster Valley pie (made with ground pork), *roïgabrageldi* (smoked meat with steamed potatoes and onion) and, of course, lots of Munster cheese.

PARMIGIANO REGGIANO

THE OPENING of a whole Parmigiano Reggiano is one of the great sights in a cheese shop. Aged for at least a year, but usually for much longer, the rock-hard 40 kg (88 lb) cheese is typically scored from top to bottom with a special hooked knife before other stubby blades are jammed in along the line and carefully levered until the cheese suddenly breaks down the middle into two huge craggy pieces with an audible crack. If it's a good cheese, the room will be filled with a gorgeous perfumed burst of pineapple and tropical fruit aromas.

What's extraordinary about this wonderful piece of cheese theatre is that it has been played out for 800 years, and probably much longer.

The first written reference to the cheese is a notary deed from 1254 in which a Genoese noblewoman traded her house for an annual supply of 53 lbs (24 kg) of Parmesan. Given that is only just over half a whole cheese by today's standard that seems a pretty bad deal, but it does show that cheeses from Parma had already achieved an illustrious

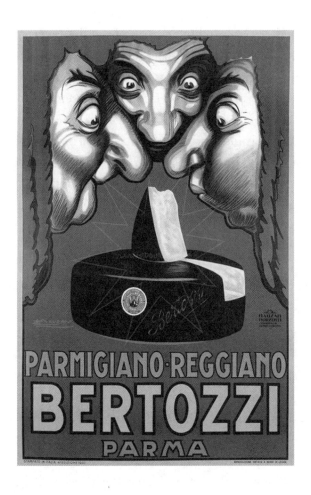

reputation and so had likely been made for decades if not centuries previously.[22]

As with so many cheeses, we have the monks to thank for the creation of Parmigiano Reggiano. After the fall of the Roman Empire, the plains of Parma, Reggio and Emilia in northern Italy, which spread along the Po river, had turned into inhospitable marshland. But from around the tenth century the region was transformed by Benedictine and Cistercian monks into farmland in a remarkable feat of human endeavour. The land, which was gifted to the monks by bishops and noblemen, was in a dire state, made up of swampy floodplains that were almost uninhabitable. By carving out canals, clearing forests and building dykes, the monks (as well as peasants coerced by local lords and town officials) were able to reclaim the land and build granges surrounded by fertile farmland for growing crops, and permanent pastures cultivated with clover and lucerne (alfalfa) as forage for cattle.[23] Digging waterways and felling entire forests by hand in the malaria-ridden back swamps of medieval Italy must have been unforgiving, back-breaking work, but they managed to completely reshape the landscape in a way that continues to benefit cheesemakers today. Newly created grazing meadows south of the river could support large herds of cows, which in turn meant lots of milk that needed storing somehow. Big cheeses that could be aged for a long time were the obvious answer, and so 'Parmigiano' (later Parmigiano-Reggiano, or Parmesan after the French word for the cheese) was born.

Quite how the monks came up with the recipe for making such a big cheese isn't known for sure. Perhaps Parmigiano was a descendent of the huge Luna cheeses made in Roman times (see Pecorino chapter). Another theory is that the know-how may have been passed on by other monks in Alpine monasteries, who had developed early forerunners of mountain cheeses such as Gruyère, Beaufort and Fontina.[24] The way Parmigiano is made is similar to these mountain cheeses. The curd is 'cooked' to high temperatures of over 50°C so that more whey is released, producing a dryer cheese for long ageing. But Parmesan is harder and grainier than Gruyère and Emmental partly because more salt is added, an ingredient that was readily available in the Po Valley from the Salsomaggiore salt mines in Parma. Indeed, Parmigiano is often described as a 'grana' cheese – a word that means 'grainy' in Italian and also gives its name to Grana Padano, a similar drum-shaped cheese also made in the Po Valley.

The hard, crystalline texture of Parmigiano makes the cheese particularly good for grating – something that was not lost on Italians in the Middle Ages. In 1344, the writer and poet Giovanni Boccaccio described a fantasy world in which people lived on a mountain of grated Parmesan cheese and 'do nought else but make macaroni and ravioli, and boil them in capon's broth' in his book *The Decameron*. Parmesan was the cheese of choice for grating over pasta during this time, according to Alberto Capatti and Massimo Montanari in their excellent book *Italian Cuisine: A Cultural History*. It was a key ingredient in lasagne, which is first mentioned in a fourteenth-century recipe book that also advises that it should be eaten with a pointed wooden tool, 'uno punctorio ligneo' – an early forerunner of the fork. In fact, Italians adopted the practice of eating with forks well before other Europeans (who ate with their hands) because of their love of molten-hot, cheesy pasta.

The fame of Parmesan soon spread well beyond Italy to become a sought-after delicacy across Europe, with large cheeses sent by barge along the river Po to the port of Venice, from where they could be shipped much further afield. In 1511, the Pope sent a gift of 100 Parmesan cheeses to King Henry VIII in return for English lead to cover St Peter's Basilica at the Vatican,[25] while legend has it that the sixteenth-century French playwright Jean Baptiste Poquelin (better known as Molière) ate 12 oz (350 g) of Parmesan and drank three glasses of Port every day during his later years. He even called for 'a little dry Parmesan' on his deathbed after collapsing on stage from pulmonary tuberculosis, managing to snaffle a piece before he went to the great stage in the sky. Parmesan was a luxury cheese that would have fetched a premium price in medieval Europe, which is why Samuel Pepys famously buried a whole 'parmezan' cheese with his fine wines in his garden to save it from the ravages of the Great Fire of London as it swept towards his house in 1666. Whether he ever dug his cheese up again, and what state it was in, was sadly never recorded in his famous diary.

The influence of the monasteries in the Po Valley declined between 1400 and 1700 as lands were expropriated

73. *Vende Form* aggio Parmigiano.

Anib. Carac. In.

by feudal lords and dukes, who also took over their cheesemaking activities. New dairies were also set up in the eighteenth century by members of the bourgeoisie and aristocratic families, who bought milk from local farms (known as the *latteroli*), but also allowed the farmers to use their dairies themselves to make their own cheese. This early spirit of cooperation developed even further in the late nineteenth century when cooperatives of farmers began setting up their own dairies, helping to boost the number of cheesemakers in the Emilia, Parma and Modena area from around 600 in 1880 to nearly 2,000 in 1922, while huge storehouses were also built to age the cheeses – a job that was taken over by specialist maturers.[26]

Eight hundred years after the monks had started to transform the landscape of the Po Valley to make cheese, the strong bonds and collective ethos of the region's cheesemakers was formalised in a voluntary organisation set up in 1928 to safeguard the cheese from imitation. This was remodelled as the Consorzio del Formaggio Parmigiano Reggiano in 1954, which soon secured a decree defining how and where the mighty cheese could be made. The Consorzio, which represents more than 3,000 dairy farms and 350 cheese dairies in the region, continues to oversee the strict PDO protecting Parmigiano Reggiano today. This specifies that it can only be made with raw milk, must be made in copper vats and must be matured for at least 12 months. It even sets out what the cows can and cannot

eat – fermented grass (silage), for example, is completely forbidden because it can lead to unwanted flavours in the cheese.

This collaborative approach, which is designed to maintain the prestige and premium prices for the benefit of everyone, is a model of success. Around 3.75 million wheels of Parmesan, equalling 150,000 tonnes of cheese, were produced in 2019 – the most that has ever been made in the cheese's long history – with around 40 per cent exported to countries all over the world. All that cheese fetched a pretty price, too. Sales were worth €2.6bn, making it the most valuable protected food in the EU. Proof that hard work, cooperation and a strong brand can turn a swamp into a goldmine.

BRIE

THE PUNGENT RIND of Munster (see previous chapter) is proof there's plenty of fun to be had with bacteria, moulds and yeasts. Get them growing in or on a cheese and they can transform its taste and texture, adding funky flavours and breaking down the paste into delicious goo. In blue cheeses, it's the mould *Penicillium roqueforti* that does the hard work (more on that later), but for soft, white cheeses it's a different strain called *Penicillium camemberti* that grows on the rind. The spores of both moulds are naturally present, and will spontaneously grow on cheeses given a chance, although cheesemakers today actually add them to the milk or rind themselves. Exactly when the transformative powers of these microbes began to be harnessed by cheesemakers is not known, but it was likely in the Middle Ages, and our friends the monks probably played an important part in refining the process in their abbey cellars.

One of the first mentions of mouldy cheese comes from a ninth-century biography of Emperor Charlemagne, which details a story of how the emperor stops at a bishop's house

where he is served an 'excellent' and 'rich and creamy' new cheese. One translation states that Charlemagne uses a knife to 'cut off the skin, which he thought unsavoury'. According to cheese historian Paul Kindstedt, this would suggest a Brie-style cheese, but fellow historian Andrew Dalby uses another interpretation of the passage that says Charlemagne 'picked out the mould, which he regarded as inedible'. Dalby argues that this makes it more likely to be a blue cheese. On such small details are cheese legends built. Indeed, Roquefort and Brie-de-Meaux both claim the story as their own. Either way, the bishop explains to Charlemagne that by cutting away the skin/mould he is throwing away the very best part of the cheese. The emperor promptly tries it and loves it so much he orders two cart-loads of the cheese to be delivered to his palace in Aix-la-Chapelle each year.

If it was Brie, then Charlemagne was not the only French royal to fall for its soft, earthy charms. The cheese has a long history of being loved by the nobility, which is perhaps due to the fact that the Brie region in Île-de-France is only 30 miles from the tables of the rich and wealthy of Paris. In 1217, Blanche de Navarre, countess of Champagne, was said to have sent 200 Brie cheeses to King Philip II so he could give them as gifts to the women in his court, while legend has it that King Louis XVI was arrested in 1791 in Varennes disguised as a servant as he fled the French revolution, partly because he spent too long stopping off for a wedge of Brie. The story goes that he even asked for the cheese as a last meal before being taken to the guillotine.

Whether any of these tales are true is hard to ascertain – there is very little documentary evidence to prove or disprove them either way. What is more sure is that Brie was skilfully used as a political pawn by the wily diplomat Talleyrand at the Congress of Vienna in 1815 – a summit of European diplomats tasked with reorganising Europe after the defeat of Napoleon. Talleyrand, who had previously been Napoleon's right-hand man, but had cannily switched sides to represent the newly restored French monarchy, was negotiating from a position of weakness. France had been defeated resoundingly in the Napoleonic wars, but the cunning politician had an ace up his sleeve: Brie-de-Meaux.

When foreign diplomats extolled the virtues of their respective countries' national cheeses over dinner one night at the conference, Talleyrand quickly challenged them to put their claims to the taste test in what was arguably the first ever global cheese contest. Around 60 cheeses were tasted in the competition organised by Talleyrand, including Stilton from England, Emmental from Switzerland, Edam from Holland and Brie-de-Meaux from a farm close to the village of Meaux. In a moment that would be worthy of a final scene in a historical blockbuster, the 52 diplomats tasted the French cheese last.

'The brie rendered its cream to the knife,' wrote the historian Jean Orieux in his biography of Talleyrand. 'It was a feast, and no one further argued the point.'[27] Brie-de-Meaux was duly crowned 'le Roi des Fromages' (the King of Cheeses) by the admiring foreign diplomats, representing a huge PR coup for Talleyrand and France. More importantly for our story, it also cemented Brie's reputation as one of the world's most famous cheeses.

Despite the cheese's aristocratic connections, Brie had humble roots. It's thought that bloomy-rinded cheeses were likely to have been first made by peasant tenant farmers as simple fresh cheeses that would naturally form white, mouldy coats as they matured in the damp cellars of northern France. Some of the cheeses would have been given to manors and monasteries as payment for rent, which would have developed the technique further in their own

cheesemaking operations. These peasant beginnings perhaps explain why Brie has a history that cuts across wealth and status. Farmers and bourgeois merchants enjoyed a wedge of Brie just as much as emperors and diplomats. This democratisation of Brie was highlighted during the French Revolution, when the revolutionary man of letters Joseph Lavallée is said to have written: 'Brie cheese, loved by rich and poor, was preaching equality before this was thought possible.'

Brie's position as cheese of the people in France was usurped in the twentieth century by a similar bloomy-rinded cow's milk fromage from Normandy. Legend has it that Camembert was first created by farmer's wife Marie

Harel in the Norman village of the same name in 1792, who agreed to shelter a young priest from the Brie region, who had fled revolutionary anti-clerical violence during the French Revolution. In return he showed her how to make a Brie-style cheese, and so Camembert was born. It's a widely quoted story, but as so often with cheese history, it's probably not true: there is historical evidence to show a cheese called Camembert was made as early 1702.[28]

Camembert became a national treasure during the First World War thanks to a marketing masterstroke dreamed up by the association representing cheesemakers in Normandy. It committed to supplying the army with one day of its members' production each week at a much reduced price, so that soldiers on the front line, nicknamed *poilus* ('hairies'), could have French cheese as part of their rations (which also included around half a litre a day of rough red wine called *pinard*). Each month around one million Camemberts were produced for the front line.

According to Pierre Boisard in his book *Camembert: A National Myth*, the cheese and wine rations were hugely important to the poilus, providing a fleeting moment of pleasure amidst the horror of war, but also holding a religious significance for the mainly Catholic soldiers because it mimicked the act of taking the Eucharist and drinking consecrated wine at church. 'A patriotic equivalent to the Catholic rite of communion, the partaking of cheap red wine and Camembert served to remind the combatants of

what they were fighting for: their land and its produce,' he wrote, before adding: 'For men who had been at the front, Camembert was a part of the mythology of the Great War.'[29]

It's a mythology that helped position Camembert as a national symbol of France, emblematic of its cultural identity. A place it continues to hold today as evidenced by the public outrage at an agreement in 2018 to loosen the PDO rules protecting unpasteurised Camembert de Normandie so that it could be made with pasteurised milk. The deal was front-page news and led to demonstrations at the French parliament and a petition signed by the country's best chefs. The fightback seems to have worked for now, with the decision overturned in 2020. Such is the power of mouldy cheese.

ROQUEFORT

As we saw with Brie, there's an awful lot of myth and legend around cheese history, which is one of the reasons why it's so much fun. Everyone loves a good shaggy cheese tale. Take Roquefort, for example. The story goes that the blue cheese from the South of France was discovered more than a thousand years ago by a lovestruck young shepherd, who left his lunch of rye bread and fresh sheep's cheese in a cave after chasing off in hot pursuit of a beautiful woman. The young Romeo returned a few weeks later to find his white cheese was covered in blue mould. He gave it a taste and it was delicious, and so Roquefort was born.

It's a great story that cheesemongers love to tell, but there is absolutely no proof to back it up. What's more, Gorgonzola has a very similar legend about a young cheesemaker. What can be said with more certainty is that Roquefort has been made from at least 1070, thanks to a charter of the same date that confirms the donation of a cheese cave and a farm by a local nobleman to the Benedictine Abbey of Conques.[30]

The cave in question was in Roquefort-sur-Soulzon in Aveyron – a village that sits beneath a huge cliff formed millions of years ago during the collapse of Mont Combalou. The landslide created a labyrinth of natural limestone caves, which are cool, damp and have a steady flow of fresh air provided by faults and cracks known as *fleurines*. It's the perfect environment for storing cheese, which is why the monks of Conques must have been delighted to be gifted one nearly a thousand years ago.

Cheesemaking was well established in the area at this time and the local shepherds and farmers, who rented land from the monks, would pay them in cheese – typically moist, salty cheeses made with milk from hardy ewes that were happy grazing the rocky landscape. Like the young shepherd in the story, the monks would have found these cheeses naturally turned blue in the damp caves of Combalou. It wasn't long before other abbeys cottoned on to the fact and also acquired caves for maturing cheese.

It was thought that the blue mould naturally grew on the rock face in the caves. Historically, cheesemakers would place pieces of rye bread among their maturing cheeses until they became covered in mould, which would then be sprinkled directly into the milk to encourage the cheeses to turn blue. However, scientific research published in 2019 has thrown some doubt on the importance of the caves when it comes to the pockets of blue that pockmark the inside of Roquefort.[31] While the humidity and cool temperature will certainly help mould to develop, analysis of different Roquefort cheeses has found that the blue mould spores are more likely to have come from the fodder eaten by the sheep, inoculating the milk before it even gets to the vat, or from the flour used to make the bread. In fact, scientists could find no *Penicillium roqueforti* at all in the caves. It turns out the shepherd's cheese would probably have turned blue if he'd left it anywhere cool and humid.

Rye bread is not widely used today either. Instead, *Penicillium roqueforti* is cultured in labs and added as a powder to the milk, but under the terms of its PDO all Roquefort cheese must still spend at least 14 days in one of the caves of Combalou.

With the monks in charge, Roquefort's reputation for piquant blues grew rapidly beyond its local market to the point where it was well known across the South of France and even further afield. In 1411 a charter signed by King Charles VI specified that Roquefort cheese could only be aged in the Combalou caves, in what is arguably the first ever 'appellation' for food in France. This protection was strengthened in 1666 by the Parliament of Toulouse, which made the trade of fake Roquefort (i.e., cheese not matured in the caves) punishable with fines, and again in 1925 when Roquefort was the first cheese to secure Appellation d'Origine Contrôlée (AOC) status – legal protection that was previously only awarded to wine and from which the EU's Protected Food Names scheme evolved.[32]

As we saw with Parmigiano Reggiano, if a cheese has a long history and a good story to tell (whether it's true or not) then it pays to protect it. Dutch cheesemakers never managed to properly enshrine in law where and how Gouda could be made. Neither did Cheddar makers in Somerset. Consequently, both cheeses can be made anywhere in the world. Around 19,000 tonnes of Roquefort are made each year, but because it is protected by a PDO the cheeses can only be made in a limited area – Aveyron, Aude, Gard, Hérault, Lozère or Tarn – using unpasteurised milk from the Lacaune breed of sheep.

Perhaps because Roquefort has been so successful at protecting its name, many other French blue cheeses have followed suit, including Bleu d'Auvergne, Bleu des Causses and Fourme d'Ambert. It's a similar story across Europe, where the most famous blue cheeses are protected, from Cabrales, a wild, spicy cave-aged blue from Asturias, to crumbly, creamy Stilton from Britain. Whether these PDOs are a good thing or not is open to debate. The principle of protecting the geographical links and traditions of ancient cheeses is admirable, but setting down strict rules on how and where a cheese is made can prevent innovation and evolution. At the same time, PDO specifications are drawn up by the cheesemakers themselves, which enables large-scale industrial manufacturers to exploit the system by pushing through watered-down specifications, allowing their cheeses to be made in factories with pasteurised milk from many farms.

Le Pape Mangeant Du fromage de rocquefort

Décret du mai 1791

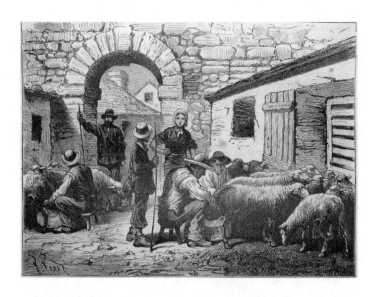

Roquefort has managed to retain its raw-milk status, but none of the seven companies that make it are true farmhouse (*fermier*) producers because they all use milk from more than one farm. In fact, around 70 per cent of all Roquefort is produced by Société des Caves, a brand owned by one of the world's biggest dairy groups, Lactalis.[33] Ironically, Lactalis has been accused of undermining its own cheese and the PDO after it launched a milder pasteurised sheep's milk fromage called Bleu de Brebis (Ewes' Blue) in 2019 in confusingly similar packaging to its own Roquefort. The move enraged agricultural and cheese worker unions, leading to demonstrations in supermarkets stocking the new cheese and threats of a legal challenge by outspoken farmer and Green MEP José Bové.[34]

Sporting a fine handlebar moustache and often seen smoking a pipe, Bové is not a man to be messed with. In 1999 he trashed a McDonald's franchise in Aveyron to protest against US restrictions on Roquefort imports, which were harming local farmers, and was sentenced to three months in prison. He's been hailed as a national hero by many in France ever since. With people like him fighting for Roquefort, the story of France's most famous blue still has a few twists in it yet.

GOUDA

It wasn't much fun being a peasant in the fourteenth and fifteenth centuries in Europe. War, famine and plague ravaged countries during the period known catchily by historians as the Crisis of the Late Middle Ages. In the four years between 1347 and 1351, when the Black Death was at its height in Europe, it's estimated that the disease killed 30 to 60 per cent of the population, amounting to more than 25 million deaths, with the poor hit particularly hard.[35] This period of terrible upheaval and hardship led to great political, religious, economic and social change over the following centuries, which saw the old feudal system of lords, manors, monks and monasteries begin to buckle under the strain. Labour shortages and popular revolts saw greater rights slowly ceded to peasants, growth in urban populations and a rise in the number of merchants and traders as market forces began to play a much bigger role in shaping societies, all of which had big repercussions for cheese.

Nowhere was this more true than the Netherlands, which went through a period known as the Dutch Golden Age during the sixteenth and seventeenth centuries, when it was envied around the world for its advances in trade, military power, science and art. More importantly for our story, it was also a fruitful time for cheesemakers.

Previously a barren marshland, the Netherlands had been reclaimed from the sea over several centuries during the Middle Ages through the construction of dykes and ditches and by using windmills to pump water from the land to create fertile fields known as polders. Much of the work was carried out by peasants on behalf of aristocratic landowners and the church, who in return granted them freedom and their own land, where they set up family dairy farms for cheese and butter production. It's estimated that in 1500 around half of all Dutch households – approximately 35,000 homes – produced butter and cheese with milk from their own cows. Typically, farms had five or six cows at this point, but as the century progressed and families profited from their hard work and could reinvest, herd sizes increased substantially so that by the seventeenth century the average herd was around twenty-five cows.[36]

More cows meant more cheese, which lead to bumper sales at markets across the country, especially in Alkmaar, Gouda and Hoorn, each of which handled several thousand tonnes of cheese each year during the seventeenth century as Holland's cheese output grew rapidly, no doubt helped by the Protestant work ethic of Calvinism, which had swept through the country. Exports were also big business, with

de WAEGH en KAES MARCKT
Van de
STADT ALCKMAER.

Schuit Van der Does
te Koop bij Adriaen Haiersou Boeckverkoper
op de
Mient jnde Witte Os

the quality of Dutch cheese admired around the world, and big demand from Britain, France and Spain.

An important transit point between Amsterdam and Rotterdam, Gouda cheese market was first set up in 1395 and had a monopoly on all cheese sales in the region. The market is still going strong today, although as a tourist attraction rather than the important commercial hub it used to be. Visit during the spring and summer and you can get a sense of what it must have been like several hundred years ago, with farmers bringing huge wheels of orange Gouda to the city's main square to sell outside the old weigh house that dates back to 1668. The cheeses are the focus of good-natured haggling between traders clad in traditional outfits, who seal deals using a series of hand slaps followed by a handshake.

Driven by the promise of more profits, Dutch cheese-makers developed innovative new cheeses with long shelf lives that could be easily transported. In the north of the country, it was the red cannonball-shaped Edam that was king, while in the south it was the disc-shaped Gouda that ruled the market. Both cheeses were pressed to reduce moisture content so they could be aged and kept for long periods, and were moulded with smooth rounded edges, which meant no sharp corners that could be damaged or cause cracking as they were shipped.

While Edam is famous today for its red wax coating, in the seventeenth century the red rind was created by rubbing it with cloths that had been soaked in a dye made by crushing seeds of the turnsole flower, which were then hung over tubs of urine. The dye would react with the ammonia from the urine and turn a vibrant violet colour, which would then be rubbed on the cheese, turning to a lustrous red when it dried. Gouda had a similar brightly coloured rind – sunshine yellow from being rubbed in vinegar infused with saffron.

New moulds and presses were developed by cheese-makers to create these cheeses for export, as well as new production techniques. Balls of Edam were submerged in hot whey to create a smooth, durable rind, while during Gouda production some of the whey would be drained from the curds and replaced with hot water in a process known today as 'washing the curd'. This helped create a drier cheese, which could be aged longer, but also gave Gouda its trademark nutty, caramel flavour.

The Dutch also developed ideas around the importance of cleanliness and hygiene, cooling milk in specially designed cold-water baths and building dairies in basements on the north side of farmhouses so that temperatures would remain chilly and constant. Once again, market forces were driving these innovations, as emphasised in a text from 1853: 'The Dutch dairyman knows perfectly well that his dairy can secure him the highest profit only when the utmost cleanliness is the basis and groundwork of his whole business,' it says in the *Dairy Husbandry of Holland*.

The text goes on to paint an evocative picture of the pristine conditions in which cheeses were transported to market by cheesemakers dressed in white linen 'cheese-frocks', with the cheeses displayed in 'glittering white linen cloth'.[37]

So proud were the Dutch of their cheeses, especially Gouda, that they were often depicted in some of the period's greatest works of art. Clara Peeters' *Still Life with Cheeses, Almonds and Pretzels*, painted in 1615, features a half wheel of Gouda, a green Edam (probably coloured with parsley) and some kind of soft cheese. It is so detailed you can see the knife cuts in the Gouda, and even a plug of cheese left by a cheese iron.

Kathryn Murphy, a fellow at the University of Oxford, argues that Dutch painters were fascinated by cheese because there was still such mystery and magic surrounding the cheesemaking process. The science of how milk was transformed into curd was still not properly understood; nor was the appearance of mites and maggots in cheese.[38] Some thought that these tiny insects were actually produced by some kind of spontaneous generation from within the cheese itself – a notion that was finally disproved when Dutch inventors developed early versions of the microscope, initially testing it on cheese rinds to discover the rather less exciting truth: cheese mites lay eggs.

A quick word on cheese mites. These tiny arthropods remain an annoying pest for many cheesemakers today. Almost invisible to the human eye, they colonise the mouldy rinds of hard, aged cheeses, burrowing into the paste and causing cracks and discolouration. They are a particular nuisance for cloth-bound-Cheddar makers, who spend an inordinate amount of time using air blowers or high-powered vacuum cleaners to get rid of the little critters. However, makers of Mimolette – a hard French cheese originally inspired by Edam – are unusual in actually encouraging cheese mites. They allow the creatures to populate the outside of the cheese in order to develop a pitted, lunar-like rind, creating unique flavours and textures in the

process. As you might expect, this is one cheese where it's probably best not to eat the rind.

Getting back to our story, the Dutch weren't alone in enjoying a bonanza of cheese production during the sixteenth and seventeenth centuries. As the Middle Ages gave way to the Age of Reason, Parmesan and Brie were both exported all over Europe as the market for foreign luxuries grew, while Gruyère from Switzerland was much in demand in France, as was Emmental, which was shipped three cheeses to a barrel.

English cheese also underwent a remarkable transformation during this period, thanks to the entrepreneurial zeal of a new class of farmers who helped create a Golden Age for one cheese in particular: Cheshire.

CHESHIRE

THE DISSOLUTION of the monasteries by Henry VIII in the sixteenth century worked out better for farmers than it did for monks. It wasn't bad for English cheeses either.

There were nearly 900 religious houses in England in 1536, but by 1541 they had all been closed and more than 12,000 monks, canons, friars and nuns were suddenly without a home. Many of the cheesemakers who had previously worked at monasteries were snapped up by local farmers, who also did well from of the great sale of monastic land and livestock that accompanied dissolution.[39]

Known as yeomen, these entrepreneurial farmers typically owned upwards of 50 acres, which they used to grow various crops and rear livestock, including cows and sheep, whose milk would be turned into cheese and butter. Over the next 300 years, they helped create and develop cheeses that are still well known today, from Cheshire and Stilton to Gloucester and Cheddar, with a similar commercial zeal to the Gouda makers on the Dutch polders.

TURKEYS' EGGS.

GORGONZOLA CHEESE.

CREAM CHEESE.

CAMEMBERT CHEESE.

BONDON CHEESE.

BALL OF BUTTER.

DUCKS' EGGS.

CURLED BUTTER.

CHEDDAR CHEESE.

PAT OF BUTTER

CHESHIRE CHEESE.

YORKSHIRE CHEESE.

STILTON CHEESE.

In the sixteenth century, it was East Anglia that was the centre of British cheesemaking, with yeoman farmers benefiting from lucrative contracts to supply cheese and butter to London cheesemongers, as well as the army and navy. The canny farmers would first skim some of the cream from the milk to make butter and then get a second bite of the cherry, using the remaining milk to make a lower-fat 'flett' cheese. The problem was that demand for butter grew so much that East Anglian cheesemakers got greedy and began to skim more and more of the cream, leaving a cheese so hard and lacking in flavour that it was mockingly nicknamed Suffolk Bang, and became the butt of many jokes. In his book *A Tour Through the Whole Island of Great Britain*, published in the 1720s, author Daniel Defoe describes Suffolk as being famous for making 'perhaps the worst cheese in the world', while one seventeenth-century proverb summed up its hard texture thus: 'Hunger will break through stone walls, and anything except a Suffolk cheese.'

Tired of cheese that blunted their teeth, London's cheesemongers started to look further afield for something a bit better for the capital's boards. The beginning of the end for Suffolk Bang came on 21 October 1650 when the cargo ship *James* arrived at the Port of London with a consignment of 20 tonnes of full-cream Cheshire cheese on board. After years of gnawing on flett cheese from East Anglia, the rich, crumbly Cheshire, made with whole milk, was immediately snapped up by cheese lovers, even though it cost a penny a pound more than East Anglian cheeses, equating to a 30 per cent premium. It marked the beginning of an amazing upturn in Cheshire's fortunes, which saw the amount of cheese shipped to London in barges and sailboats known as 'ketches' increase from almost nothing in 1650 to 2,000 tonnes in the 1680s and 5,766 tonnes by 1729. By contrast, only 985 tonnes of the once dominant Suffolk cheese arrived in London 1729, marking a serious fall from grace.[40]

As these figures suggest, the entrepreneurial yeomen of Cheshire didn't hang about when it came to scaling up production. Farms and herd sizes were increased by merging smaller operations together, enclosing common land, and by renting pastures from other landowners, while new techniques for growing better pasture were introduced. Cheese sizes also increased from an average weight of 12 lbs (5.5 kg) in 1664 to nearly 20 lbs (9 kg) in 1699 so that they were less likely to dry out on the journey to London, and would arrive still crumbly and moist.[41] By the mid-eighteenth century, Cheshires could weigh up to 60 lbs (27 kg) – a size so big that new ways of cheesemaking were introduced, including new, heavier presses to squeeze out more of the whey, and adding salt to the broken-up curd before it was moulded so the cheeses wouldn't rot at their core as they matured. The outsides were also rubbed with melted butter and later sealed with cloth to create a durable rind. Some of these techniques were adopted by cheesemakers in other regions of England, too, including Lancashire, Gloucestershire and Leicestershire, while the eighteenth century saw new styles of cheese attracting the attentions of buyers (known as cheese factors).

Stilton came to prominence in the early eighteenth century, named after the Cambridgeshire village where it was served at the Bell Inn – an important staging post on the Great North Road – although cheese historians keep falling out with each other over whether it was ever actually made there. It's also not clear whether Stilton was the creamy, crumbly blue of today or a hard, aged cheese more like a Parmesan or, indeed, a spreadable cream cheese. Daniel Defoe wrote at the time that the cheese was 'brought to the table with the mites, or maggots round it, so thick that they bring a spoon with them for you to eat the mites with as you do the cheese,' which doesn't really throw much light on the matter, beyond making the cheese sound pretty much inedible.

Stilton continues to be held in high regard today, but Cheshire's place as the nation's favourite cheese was slowly eroded over time by a cheese from Somerset that went on to take over the world. As we will see in the next chapter, Cheddar went from being a niche regional cheese in the nineteenth century to a global, industrialised behemoth in an amazingly short space of time, leaving Cheshire trailing in its wake.

Cheshire's decline in the twentieth century was spectacular, with the number of farms producing the cheese falling from more than 2,000 in 1900 to just 40 following the Second World War, with the vast majority of production concentrated in large-scale creameries.[42] Factory-made

Cheshire, which is young, acidic and bland, is what is found on most supermarket shelves these days – a pale shadow of what the mighty cheese used to be. Thankfully there are still two farms left in the UK making old-style Cheshire: Appleby's and H. S. Bourne, which use raw milk to create cloth-bound cheeses that are very different to modern versions. Flaky, zesty and with a complex savoury finish, they're worth seeking out.

CHEDDAR

CHEDDAR WAS well known in the seventeenth century, but was a rare sight outside its home county of Somerset, partly because the cheeses were so huge. Each village would pool its milk to make a single vast truckle that could weigh well over 100 lbs (45 kg), a size that made it difficult to transport, but excellent for ageing into a complex, mature cheese. In Defoe's chapter on 'Somersetshire' in his *A Tour Through the Whole Island of Great Britain*, he noted that Cheddar was 'the best cheese that England affords, if not, that the whole world affords'.

This stellar reputation was matched by its price, with Cheddar costing around three times the price of Cheshire in the seventeenth century. It was seen as a luxury cheese for the rich and aristocratic, with most bought before it had even been made. But as road and canal networks improved towards the end of the eighteenth century, Cheddar became more available and slowly began to rival Cheshire as the cheese of choice in Britain. It was helped on its way by advances in animal breeding, which led to cows such as the

Dairy Shorthorn that produced abundant amounts of good milk, while improvements in pasture and animal feed were matched by more efficient cheesemaking equipment, from new vats to specialist curd knives.

Cheese production in the UK grew from an estimated 75,000 tonnes in 1800 to 90,000 tonnes in 1850 as farming and production became more sophisticated.[43] To demonstrate just how skilled cheesemaking was in this period a group of Cheddar makers in Pennard, near Glastonbury, decided to make a cheese weighing half a tonne as a gift for Queen Victoria to celebrate her marriage to Prince Albert in 1840. According to newspaper reports from the time, nearly 50 dairymaids used the milk of 737 cows to make the cheese, which was formed in a specially designed octagonal mould made from five-inch-thick Spanish mahogany.[44] After being presented to the Queen, the cheese was shown to the public on a tour round the country. Whether Victoria actually got to try it and what it tasted like has unfortunately been lost to history.

One of the most influential figures in the history of Cheddar was Joseph Harding – dubbed 'the father of Cheddar' because of his pioneering work to push the boundaries of scientific knowledge and dairy hygiene in cheesemaking. Harding and his wife, Rachel, who made cheese at their farm in Marksbury, Somerset, set about developing a defined system of Cheddar making in the 1850s to help improve consistency and quality. By experimenting with their own cheese and visiting other Cheddar makers the couple devised an empirical approach, known as the 'Harding method', based on monitoring temperature, timings and acidity levels, as well as stressing the importance of clean milk and good dairy hygiene. 'Cheese is not made in the field, nor in the byre, nor even in the cow, it is made in the dairy,' said Harding,[45] who described the ideal Cheddar as 'Close and firm in texture, yet mellow in character or quality; it is rich with a tendency to melt in the mouth, the flavour full and fine, approaching to that of a hazelnut.'[46]

Harding outlined his method in a series of articles, and he and Rachel taught cheesemaking classes around the country, and also welcomed delegations of cheesemakers from Scotland, Denmark and the US. While this spreading of cheese knowledge was admirable, it eventually came back to bite Somerset Cheddar makers in an unexpected way. US dairyman Xerxes Willard, who visited Harding in 1866, used his method to bolster his country's burgeoning network of Cheddar factories. This development eventually saw cheap American Cheddar exported to the UK, much to the detriment of British cheesemakers.

Cheesemaking had been established in the US by Puritan colonies in New England in the early seventeenth century, and by the time Willard visited Somerset to learn Harding's Cheddar secrets, the US was well on the way to scaling up cheese production. The world's first ever

cheese factory was set up in New York State in 1851 by a dairy farmer called Jesse Williams, who pooled the milk of 300–400 cows from neighbouring farms to make around 100,000 lbs (45,000 kg) of Cheddar a year – more than five times what a typical individual farm could produce. The idea caught on and by 1861 there were twenty-one cheese factories in operation in the state, working to a similar cooperative model around a central dairy. By 1899 there were around 1,500 cheese factories across the US, most of them making Cheddar.[47]

The US exported around 2,000 tonnes of cheese to Britain in 1860. By 1881 it was an incredible 67,000 tonnes.

Willard himself admitted that US Cheddar wasn't as complex or delicious as the traditional farmhouse cheese produced by Harding, which he praised for having a 'fine delicate flavour', but it was significantly cheaper and consistent enough for London cheesemongers to choose American (and later Canadian and Australian) over British.

Cheese factories did also open in England – the first on the Longford Estate in Derbyshire in 1870 – but they struggled to make an impact, mainly because it was more profitable and easier for farms to sell liquid milk into the cities on the newly opened railway lines that began to criss-cross the country. It all added up to a massive fall in cheese production in Britain. Volumes fell by around 60 per cent between 1850 and 1908, and it's estimated that around 80 per cent of all the cheese eaten in Britain in 1913 was imported.

Farmhouse Cheddar and Cheshire production in Britain struggled on in the twentieth century, but continued to be degraded by competition from cheap foreign imports. Other factors also had a detrimental impact, including the devastation of the First World War and the creation of the Milk Marketing Board in 1933, which set milk quotas, guaranteeing farmers decent returns for liquid milk and giving little incentive to make cheese. Rationing in Britain during the Second World War, which didn't stop until 1954, also had destructive consequences: in an effort to feed the nation, cheesemaking was centralised, with only certain types allowed to be made, most notoriously 'Government Cheddar' – a bland, flavourless creation that was scornfully nicknamed 'mousetrap cheese'.

Of the 514 farms making cheese in the southwest of England in 1939, only 57 were still in production when the Second World War ended in 1945.[48] The second half of the twentieth century saw British Cheddar dominated by large factory operations producing rindless block cheeses with pasteurised milk from multiple farms, which were aged in plastic so no moisture was lost, giving the final cheese a squidgy texture. It's a situation that remains the same today, with just four farmhouse raw-milk Cheddar makers left in Somerset.

It's a similar story in the US, where the cheese market has continued to be dominated by factories, producing block Cheddar as well as that all-American staple: processed cheese. A blend of ground cheese (often Cheddar), emulsifiers and dairy powders, heated into a homogeneous goo, processed cheese is famously shaped into fluorescent orange slices for melting on burgers. It was invented by James L. Kraft in 1916, who first packaged it in cans and sold 25 million of them to the US army during the First World War. Today Kraft (which merged with Heinz in 2015) has a $26bn turnover and operates in more than 40 countries, proving that there is plenty of profit in cheese goo.

Cheddar's journey from hidden Somerset gem to multibillion-dollar global commodity is an extreme example of how cheese became industrialised in the twentieth century. But at the turn of the twenty-first century small-scale cheesemakers mounted a spirited fightback, marking a revival in artisan cheese. Most surprising of all was that US cheesemakers were at the vanguard of this new movement.

ROGUE RIVER BLUE

THE WORLD CHEESE AWARDS have been crowning the best cheeses on the planet every year since 1988, but it was the 2019 competition that was arguably the most dramatic. And not just because there was a record number of entries: 3,804 cheeses from more than 40 countries, filling a football pitch-sized exhibition hall in Bergamo, Italy.

After a morning in which 250 expert judges sniffed, poked and tasted their way through all the cheeses in a series of blind judgings, the field was narrowed down to just two, tied on 100 points. One was clearly a Parmigiano Reggiano; the other was much harder to recognise. A soft blue cheese wrapped in vine leaves, it had a roller coaster flavour that took in everything from notes of pear and vanilla to bacon and spice.

The Parmesan was not surprisingly the favourite among the crowd of several hundred expectant Italians, but to their consternation it was the mysterious blue that narrowly took the coveted title of 'best cheese in the world' after a tense final tasting.

The disappointment that the Italians felt turned to disbelief and a certain level of outrage when it was revealed the winner wasn't even made in Europe, but was in fact an American cheese, called Rogue River Blue. Newspaper articles over the following weeks questioned how a country known for making plastic orange burger cheese could possibly beat the best in Europe to win the top prize. The answer was that unbeknownst to many in the Old World, the US cheese industry had undergone a revolution in the previous twenty years, with a big jump in the number of cheesemakers going back to the traditional techniques first brought by the founding fathers.

Interest in where food came from and how it was made flourished in the US in the 2000s, with a big rise in restaurants, celebrity-chef cookery shows, farmers' markets and independent food shops. A corresponding jump in the number of artisan cheesemakers saw membership of the American Cheese Society, which represents small-scale producers, double in a decade to nearly 2,100 members in 2020.[49]

Rogue Creamery in Oregon is one of this new breed, albeit with a longer history than most. Located in the beautiful Rogue Valley and owned by the Vella family since the 1930s, the company was bought by former product development and branding executive David Gremmels and his partner Cary Bryant in 2002, who transformed its fortunes with a commitment to organic farming practices

and innovative new products. Rogue River Blue was developed to reflect the terroir of Oregon, using milk from the company's 120-strong herd of Holstein and Brown Swiss cows to make a blue cheese that is aged for a year and wrapped in Syrah vine leaves from a nearby biodynamic vineyard, which are macerated in pear spirit, another local speciality. The cheese is only made for a few months each year, between the Autumnal Equinox and the Winter Solstice, when cooler temperatures and high-quality pastures mean richer milk. This focus on quality and provenance is a common thread among artisan cheesemakers in the US, who are able to sell their products at premium prices (Rogue River retails for around $50 per pound) in top-end restaurants and specialist retailers such as Whole Foods Market and Murray's, where hip young mongers, often sporting cheese and cow tattoos, preach the benefits of good cheese with an almost religious fervour.

According to a report commissioned in 2019 by the Vermont Agency of Agriculture, the entire US cheese industry was valued at $18bn in 2018, with 'specialty' cheese (as the market is known in the US) accounting for $4.2bn of that. What's more, sales of specialty cheese were growing five times faster than the overall cheese category.

There's been a similar revival in other countries where large-scale cheesemaking has dominated. Australia, Spain and Ireland have all seen a resurgence in artisan cheese-making, as has the UK, where the Specialist Cheesemakers

Association has seen membership grow to more than 200 producers, making more than 700 different cheese varieties. To put that in perspective, in the 1970s when farmhouse cheese production was at its nadir, there were only 62 farms making cheese. That last figure comes from *The Great British Cheese Book*, by Patrick Rance, published in 1982, who helped spearhead the artisan cheese recovery in the UK. A flamboyant figure who was often seen sporting a rather fine monocle, Rance was a former major in the army, who fought in the Second World War, before taking over Wells Stores in Streatley, Berkshire, in 1954 and entering a new battle to save traditional, raw-milk cheeses from the march of factory-made products. 'Your clamorous protests alone can save our Real Cheese from being lost forever in the rising flood of plastic-smothered insipidity,' he wrote in the stirring preface to his seminal work.

Rance was joined in his crusade by others, including Randolph Hodgson, who co-founded groundbreaking cheese shop Neal's Yard Dairy in Covent Garden in 1979. Their cause was helped when the Milk Marketing Board's powers to set milk prices were ended in 1994, sparking a slump in prices. Dairy farmers soon started to add value to their milk by making cheese again, helping to swell cheesemaker numbers. A wave of British artisan cheeses hit the market over the following decades with fresh takes on traditional territorials, such as Caerphilly, Cheddar and Wensleydale, as well as a huge number of completely new cheeses that took inspiration from Continental classics, but had their own unique British characters.

In many ways the almost total annihilation of farmhouse cheesemaking in the US and UK has given new-wave producers the freedom to take their cheeses in interesting new directions. In Italy and France, where traditional cheesemaking never suffered in the same way, innovation is often constrained by traditions. If you are born into a family making world-famous PDO-protected Comté, the chances are you will carry on making Comté when you take over from your parents. If you are starting from scratch in the UK or US, however, you are much more likely to take inspiration from various places and create something completely new. Something like Rogue River Blue, which David Gremmels fully admits was inspired by travelling through Europe and tasting the kind of traditional regional cheeses that have featured in the chapters of this book.

While the dynamism and energy of countries such as the UK and US is encouraging, artisan cheese remains a small part of the market. The vast majority of cheese consumed around the world is made in large factories, and even in bastions of traditional production, such as Italy and France, small producers are being forced to close because of intense pressure from the supermarkets on price and competition from large producers. Around 50 varieties of French cheese have disappeared altogether in the past four decades, according to the campaign group Association Fromages de Terroirs.

The success of artisan cheese in the US has also attracted the attention of large multinationals, who have started buying up smaller cheesemakers so they can benefit from the huge growth in sales in that sector. Pioneers of the American cheese revival, such as Cowgirl Creamery, Cyprus Grove Chevre and Vermont Creamery, have all been taken over by much larger global concerns in the past decade. Rogue River Blue is part of this story. Although David Gremmels remains in charge of the day-to-day running of the business, he signed a 'partnership' deal with French dairy multinational Savencia in 2018, so he could ramp up production.

Where the cheese story goes next is hard to predict. Small cheesemakers being tempted by offers from larger competitors is nothing new, but the power of big dairy multinationals today is so all-encompassing that it makes life increasingly difficult for traditional, artisan producers. At the same time, population growth, environmental crisis and the long-term impact of the coronavirus pandemic, which was only just starting to unfold as this book was finished, will also have an impact on the ways in which cheesemakers go about their business.

Despite these challenges, there's no doubt that cheese will endure thanks to its special place in our hearts. From the first curd in the Fertile Crescent to the new wave of modern American creations, we've had an 8,000-year love affair with fermented milk that shows no sign of abating. Flavours, textures and appearances may change in the future, but cut a wedge from a good cheese and it will always provide a delicious slice of history, geography and culture.

THE PHILOSOPHY OF THE CHEESEBOARD

ACCORDING TO conventional wisdom, a cheeseboard should showcase different milk types, shapes, textures, colours and flavours. It's why the three-cheese board, comprising a hard, soft and blue, is a classic. Add in a few more – a fresh goat's cheese log and a stinky washed-rind cheese, perhaps – and you have a more lavish board with something for almost everyone.

But once you know these basic rules, you can ignore them and do what you like. A huge hunk of Stilton in the centre of the table, with walnuts and fruit cake, makes an epic cheese course. There's something rather special about venerating a single cheese in this way, giving you the time and space to really get under the rind and appreciate its complex flavours and texture. Likewise, there is great fun to be had with one style of cheese on a board, exploring the differences and similarities between, say, three of four wrinkly goat's cheeses or half a dozen mountain cheeses.

Eating seasonally is also satisfying. Goat's and sheep's milk cheeses are at their best in the spring and summer, while powerful blues and washed rinds feel better suited to the autumn and winter. But if you want to have goat's curd on Christmas day and a gooey slab of Stinking Bishop while watching Glastonbury, then that is fine too.

One last important point. The question that people always ask, apart from what's your favourite cheese (Kirkham's Lancashire), is: 'When do you eat the rind?' My answer is the same every time. Give it a go. If it tastes bad, then don't eat it, but it won't hurt you to try. The only exception is Gorgonzola. The makers of the Italian blue are unique in advising people not to eat the rind for food safety reasons, and watch out for waxed cheeses and those that have been coated in a thin plastic layer, for obvious reasons. I personally wouldn't eat the dry, dusty rind of Comté or Gruyère, or the granite-like exterior of Parmesan, but you might like to chew on them. Often the rind and the layer just beneath is where you'll find lots of interesting textures and intense flavours – this is especially true of soft, bloomy-rinded cheeses like Brie, and washed rinders such as Munster. There's no harm in trying.

HOW TO SERVE AND STORE

I'm with the French on serving cheese before pudding. It makes sense to me to keep all the savoury courses together before moving onto something sweet. I also worry that if I have dessert first, I might not have room for cheese. That doesn't bear thinking about.

That said, I also quite like eating cheese before dinner as a kind of aperitif. The Spanish start most meals with a few slices of Manchego and a glass of sherry, which I think is very civilised.

Whenever you decide to serve your cheese, it's important to get it up to room temperature. Cold kills flavour, so like a good red wine you want to make sure your cheese has opened up a bit before you eat it. An hour or so out of the fridge should be plenty of time.

While we're on the subject of fridges, it's worth pointing out that most domestic fridges are harsh environments for cheeses. Maturing cellars and caves have a constant, cool temperature, high humidity and very gentle air flow, but home fridges tend to aggressively circulate cold air, which quickly dries out cheeses if they are not protected.

I try to create a mini cave in my fridge by storing cheese in one of the salad drawers at the bottom (I remove all the salad from it first!), which protects it from the worst of the air flow. If you want to get really nerdy you can even place a clean, slightly damp cloth in the drawer to provide a little humidity.

In terms of wrapping, waxed paper is best for most cheeses, from runny Brie to flinty Parmigiano Reggiano, which is why it's the covering of choice for most cheesemongers and delis.

This leads me on nicely to where to buy cheese. I would always recommend going to a specialist cheese shop or a counter in a deli or farm shop. Most of the time the shopkeeper will let you try the cheese before you buy, will have really good knowledge and will know how to look after cheeses properly.

Most of the big supermarkets tend to work with large industrial cheese producers, rather than small, farmhouse makers, because factory-made products fit their distribution model and prices can be kept low. But it is artisan producers that invariably make the most complex, interesting and delicious cheeses. A slice of raw-milk, farmhouse Cheddar from Somerset has remarkable layers of flavour that develop and linger in a way that a piece of plastic-wrapped block Cheddar does not.

BEYOND CHUTNEY

I love ripping up the rulebook when it comes to what to serve with cheese. Yes, crackers and chutney are great, but there are plenty of other matches that can take a cheeseboard to thrilling new places.

A drizzle of honey, boozy cherries and a few roasted hazelnuts are great accompaniments, bringing sweetness, acidity and crunch. But the same is true of chocolate, pickled cabbage and even peanut brittle, all of which I've matched very successfully with cheese down the years.

You can break cheese matching down into three basic categories: pairings that have flavours that complement each other, such as a savoury Cheddar with savoury bacon jam; those that contrast, like sweet fudge and salty blue cheese; and then a final 'curve ball' category, which are completely unexpected – think Caerphilly and dark chocolate.

I particularly love to serve cheese with cake. Lancashire and Eccles cake, Cheshire on a hot cross bun, and Gorgonzola Dolce with a slice of ginger cake are all wonderful – the fruity spice of the cakes works in a similar way to chutney.

PERFECT PAIRINGS

The same principles apply to pairing drinks with cheese. There's more to life than red wine. In fact, controversial as this might sound, red wine can often be quite a tough match for cheese. The tannins in full-bodied reds clash horribly with creamy cheeses, doing neither any favours.

The acidity of white wine is a much easier pairing in my experience, cutting across the cheese so that you are ready for another bite. Sparkling wines work beautifully in this way too – the bubbles really invigorate the palate, especially with lemony soft goat's cheeses and Brie-style cheeses. At the other end of the scale, sweet wines contrast nicely with salty cheeses, especially blues.

Some of my favourite booze and cheese combos don't involve wine at all. Beer is a firm friend to most cheeses thanks to its refreshing carbonation and bitterness, while cider works for similar reasons.

In fact, there isn't a drink, alcoholic or not, that can't be enhanced with a sliver of good cheese. Sake, sherry, whisky and sloe gin are all lovely with the right cheese, as are apple juice, mocktails and even black coffee, which works surprisingly well with a slice of goat's Gouda.

If you're going to break the rules, break them properly.

FURTHER READING

Pierre Boisard, translated by Richard Miller, *Camembert: A National Myth* (California: University of California Press, 2003)

Andrew Dalby, *Cheese: A Global History* (London: Reaktion Books, 2009)

Catherine Donnelly (ed.), *The Oxford Companion to Cheese* (New York: Oxford University Press, 2016)

Paul Kindstedt, *Cheese and Culture: A History of Cheese and its Place in Western Civilization* (Vermont: Chelsea Green Publishing, 2012)

Ned Palmer, *A Cheesemonger's History of the British Isles* (London: Profile Books, 2019)

Bronwen and Francis Percival, *Reinventing the Wheel: Milk, Microbes and the Fight for Real Cheese* (London: Bloomsbury Sigma, 2017)

Patrick Rance, *The Great British Cheese Book* (London: Macmillan, 1982); *The French Cheese Book* (London: Macmillan, 1989)

I II III

IV V VI

VII VIII IX

X XI XII

LIST OF ILLUSTRATIONS

98

ENDNOTES

1 Patrick Rance, *The French Cheese Book* (London: Macmillan, 1989), p.xv

2 Graeme Barker, *The Agricultural Revolution in Prehistory: Why Did Foragers Become Farmers?* (Oxford: Oxford University Press, 2006), p.137

3 Richard Evershed, et al., 'Earliest Date for Milk Use in the Near East and Southeastern Europe Linked to Cattle Herding' (*Nature* 455, 528–531, 2008)

4 Peter Bogucki, 'Ceramic Sieves of the Linear Pottery Culture and their Economic Implications' (*Oxford Journal of Archaeology*, vol 3, issue 1: pp.15–30, 1984)

5 Melanie Salque, Peter Bogucki, Joanna Pyzel, et al., 'Earliest Evidence for Cheese Making in the Sixth Millennium BC in Northern Europe' (*Nature* 493, 522–525, 2013), https://doi.org/10.1038/nature11698

6 Jessica Hendy, Penny Bickle, Mike Copper, Sophy Charlton, 'Neolithic Cheese Making: Experimental Archaeology and Public Engagement with Replica Vessels' (*Past*, the newsletter of the Prehistoric Society, Autumn 2016)

7 Yuval Itan, et al., 'The Origins of Lactase Persistence in Europe' (*PLOS Computational Biology*, 28 August 2009)

8 Roz Gillis, 'Beyond the Pail: Archaeozoological Research into Understanding Prehistoric Milking Practises' in *May Contain Traces of Milk* (York: University of York, 2012)

9 Andrew Dalby, *Cheese: A Global History* (London: Reaktion Books, 2009), p.37

10 Paul Kindstedt, *Cheese and Culture: A History of Cheese and its Place in Western Civilization* (Vermont: Chelsea Green Publishing, 2012), p.26

11 Enrico Greco, et al, 'Proteomic Analyses on an Ancient Egyptian Cheese and Biomolecular Evidence of Brucellosis' (*Analytical Chemistry*, vol 90, issue 16, 2018)

12 Paul Kindstedt, *Cheese and Culture: A History of Cheese and its Place in Western Civilization* (Vermont: Chelsea Green Publishing, 2012), pp.45–47

13 Samuel Butler (trans), Homer's *The Odyssey* (Project Gutenberg Ebook, 1999)

14 J. M. Edmonds (trans), *Lyra Graeca* (Maryland: Wildside Press, 2007) p.83

15 https://warwick.ac.uk/fac/arts/classics/intranets/students/modules/greekreligion/database/clunbe, accessed 06/05/20

16 Oliver Craig, et al, 'Feeding Stonehenge: Cuisine and Consumption at the Late Neolithic site of Durrington Walls' (Cambridge University Press, 2015)

17 Yimin Yang, et al., 'Proteomics Evidence for Kefir Dairy in Early Bronze Age China' (*Journal of Archaeological Science*, vol 45, issue 12, 2013)

18 Paul Kindstedt, *Cheese and Culture: A History of Cheese and its Place in Western Civilization* (Vermont: Chelsea Green Publishing, 2012), p.107

19 Patrick Rance, *The French Cheese Book* (London: Macmillan, 1989), p.278

20 C. H. Lawrence, *Medieval Monasticism: Forms of Religious Life in Western Europe in the Middle Ages* (New York: Longman, 1984)

21 Fromage de Munster, http://www.munster.alsace/gastrono mie_fromage.aspx, accessed 06/05/20

22 Parmesan Cheese History, https://parmesan.com/history/ history-of-parmigiano-reggiano/, accessed 06/05/20

23 Kees de Roest, *The Production of Parmigiano-Reggiano Cheese* (Assen: Van Gorcum, 2000), pp.20–21

24 Paul Kindstedt, *Cheese and Culture: A History of Cheese and its Place in Western Civilization* (Vermont: Chelsea Green Publishing, 2012), p.156

25 Catherine Fletcher, *Diplomacy in Renaissance Rome: The Rise of the Resident Ambassador* (Cambridge: Cambridge University Press, 2015)

26 Kees de Roest, *The Production of Parmigiano-Reggiano Cheese* (Assen: Van Gorcum, 2000), p.25

27 Jean Orieux, *Talleyrand: The Art of Survival* (New York: Knopf, 1974)

28 Pierre Boisard, translated by Richard Miller, *Camembert: A National Myth* (California, University of California Press, 2003)

29 *Ibid*. p.113

30 Dick Whittaker and Jack Goody, 'Rural Manufacturing in the Rouergue from Antiquity to the Present: The Examples of Pottery and Cheese' (*Comparative Studies in Society and History*, vol 43, issue 2, 2001)

31 Emilie Dumas, et al., 'Independent Domestication Events in the Blue Cheese Fungus *Penicillium roqueforti*' (*Molecular Ecology*, 2020)

32 Roquefort, Fromages AOP, https://www.fromages-aop.com/wp-content/uploads/Roquefort-1.pdf

33 Henry Samuel, 'Roquefort Row: Purists Turn Air Blue Over Pasteurised Rival to France's "King" of Cheeses' (*The Telegraph*, 21 October 2019)

34 *Ibid.*

35 Sharon N. DeWitte, 'Black Death Bodies' (*Fragments Journal*, Michigan Publishing, vol 6, 2017)

36 Bas van Bavel and Oscar Gelderblom, 'The Economic Origins of Cleanliness in the Dutch Golden Age' (*Past & Present*, vol 205, issue 1, 2009)

37 Ellerbrock, translated by Charles Louis Flint, *Milch Cows and Dairy Farming* (Boston, Phillips, Sampson and Company, 1859), p.301

38 Kathryn Murphy, 'More to Cheese than Meets the Eye?' (*Apollo Magazine*, 11 March 2017)

39 George W. Bernard, 'The Dissolution of the Monasteries' (*History*, vol 96, no. 4, 2011)

40 Charles F. Foster, *Cheshire Cheese and Farming in the North West in the 17th & 18th Centuries* (Cheshire; Arley Hall Press, 1998)

41 *Ibid.*

42 Patrick Rance, *The Great British Cheese Book* (London: Macmillan, 1982), p.59

43 Nigel White, *The Evolution of the British Cheese Industry* (Shropshire, Society of Dairy Technology, 2018)

44 Report in *The Literary Gazette: A Weekly Journal of Literature, Science, and the Fine Arts* (London: Robson, Levey, Franklyn, 1841), p.189

45 Quoted in a lecture by Richard Bannister, published in the *Journal of the Society for Arts*, vol 36, no. 1866 (Royal Society for the Encouragement of Arts, Manufactures and Commerce, 1888)

46 Bronwen Percival, entry on Cheddar in *The Oxford Companion to Cheese* edited by Catherine Donnelly (New York: Oxford University Press, 2016)

47 Nigel White, *The Evolution of the British Cheese Industry* (Shropshire, Society of Dairy Technology, 2018)

48 Patrick Rance, *The Great British Cheese Book* (London: Macmillan, 1982), pp.8, 59

49 https://www.cheesesociety.org/about-us/, accessed 06/05/20

Also available in this series

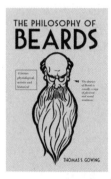

THE PHILOSOPHY OF
BEARDS

A treatise
physiological,
artistic and
historical

The absence
of Beard is
usually a sign
of physical
and mental
weakness.

THOMAS S. GOWING

THE PHILOSOPHY OF
COFFEE

BRIAN WILLIAMS

THE PHILOSOPHY OF
WINE

RUTH BALL

THE PHILOSOPHY OF
TEA

TONY GEBELY

THE PHILOSOPHY OF
BEER

JANE PEYTON

THE PHILOSOPHY OF
GIN

JANE PEYTON